BOSS WOMEN

Seven African-American Women Who Built Their Businesses From the Ground Up

Gwen Richardson

Boss Women

FIRST EDITION
Cover design by Staci Creekmore

ISBN:

978-1-7374496-1-4

Printed in the United States of America

Facebook: @bosswomenthebook
Email: gwenrichardson123@gmail.com
Website: www.gwenrichardson.com

To tomorrow's Boss Women
of future generations

You've heard of moguls Oprah and Hughes
Whose successes are shown on the evening news.
But there are other women from near and far
Who are building their empires and raising the bar.

From airplanes to houses to hygiene to hair,
They treat their clients with the greatest of care.
They're fearless, they're nimble, they're classy, they're dope
And give future generations immeasurable hope.

Some started with nothing and went to the top.
Others spent years to develop ideas and didn't stop.
Education was key and shouldn't be dismissed.
They learned all they could; they had to persist.

They've all broken barriers in some form or other
And made family proud, especially their mothers.
There are thousands of boss women on this side of heaven,
But on the pages that follow, you'll meet only seven.

Janice Adams
JMA Solutions

Her first jobs were with two very large companies.
General Motors and General Electric paid pretty good money,
But layoffs and divorce could make her home life unstable.
Janice Adams knew she had to put everything on the table.

So she joined the Armed Forces at age twenty-seven.
She selected the Air Force as her chosen profession.
To raise her two children with the support of her mother,
She rose through the ranks, up one tier then another.

After twenty-four years she decided to retire
To work as a contractor; her skills were for hire.
Her vision led her to choose aviation
And provide air traffic controllers for government locations.

JMA Solutions has a host of federal clients.
Her insistence on excellence has caused her to triumph.
And her list of awards is too long to name—
She was even inducted into the D.C. Hall of Fame.

Valerie Daniels-Carter
V&J Holdings

One of the largest female franchisees
That America's seen, and it's hard to believe
V&J Holdings was founded by Valerie.
Her last name's Daniels-Carter; she exudes vitality.

Her restaurants sell burgers, coffee, pretzels, and pizza.
Whatever you want, she's determined to feed ya.
Pizza Hut, Burger King, Captain D's, and more,
After decades in business, she's seen her profits soar.

But she doesn't limit herself to financial opportunities.

She also gives back to her local community.

Part-owner of the Milwaukee Bucks, her share is minority.

She's active in church and believes in philanthropy.

She attributes her success to her faith in God.

She offers this advice and it's not a façade:

An attitude to win is what is required

To accomplish your goals and achieve your desires.

Bea Dixon
Honey Pot

The concept for Honey Pot was revealed in a dream

Her ancestors spoke—"Heal thyself" was their theme.

For years Bea had struggled with a recurring infection.

She tried many different formulas, mixing them to perfection.

It took $20,000 to get Honey Pot started.

Brother Sy joined in and her new course was charted.

She took six hundred bottles to Atlanta for a hair show.

Then Whole Foods called; her company started to grow.

She added items like wipes and pads to her line.
Soon they were in Target—Honey Pot was nationwide.
But Bea has experienced her fair share of drama.
Folks throwin' shade, they tried to cause trauma.

But sistahs all over then flocked to Bea's side.
They gave her support, they were bursting with pride
Because finally they had what every woman needs,
Feminine products that are safe, natural, and
sulfate-free.

Janice Bryant Howroyd
ActOne Group

One of 11 children in Tarboro, North Carolina
Her parents worked hard so their lives could be finer.
Janice launched her business with a fax machine and a phone
After her mother provided her with a $900 loan.

The ActOne Group started in 1978.
The company grew quickly with the aim to innovate.
In twenty-two countries, competing with the best,
One look at their talent pool and you'll be impressed.

The ActOne Group provides employees, staffers, and talent

With cutting-edge human resources solutions that run the gamut.

From utilities to energy to broadband to tech,

With thousands employed, they continue to stretch.

According to Forbes, Janice is worth several million

The first black woman to run a company worth a billion

Seventeen thousand clients all over the world

An incredible journey for a true Southern girl.

Garnetta Sanders
Neta Scientific

Family-owned in Hainesport, New Jersey,

Nominated by Pfizer, who considered them worthy,

Garnetta's company was named subcontractor of the year.

The Small Business Administration made that abundantly clear.

The name of her firm is Neta Scientific.

With husband Winfred by her side, their success has been terrific,

Started in 1999, the end of a millennium,

With attention to detail keeping errors to a minimum.

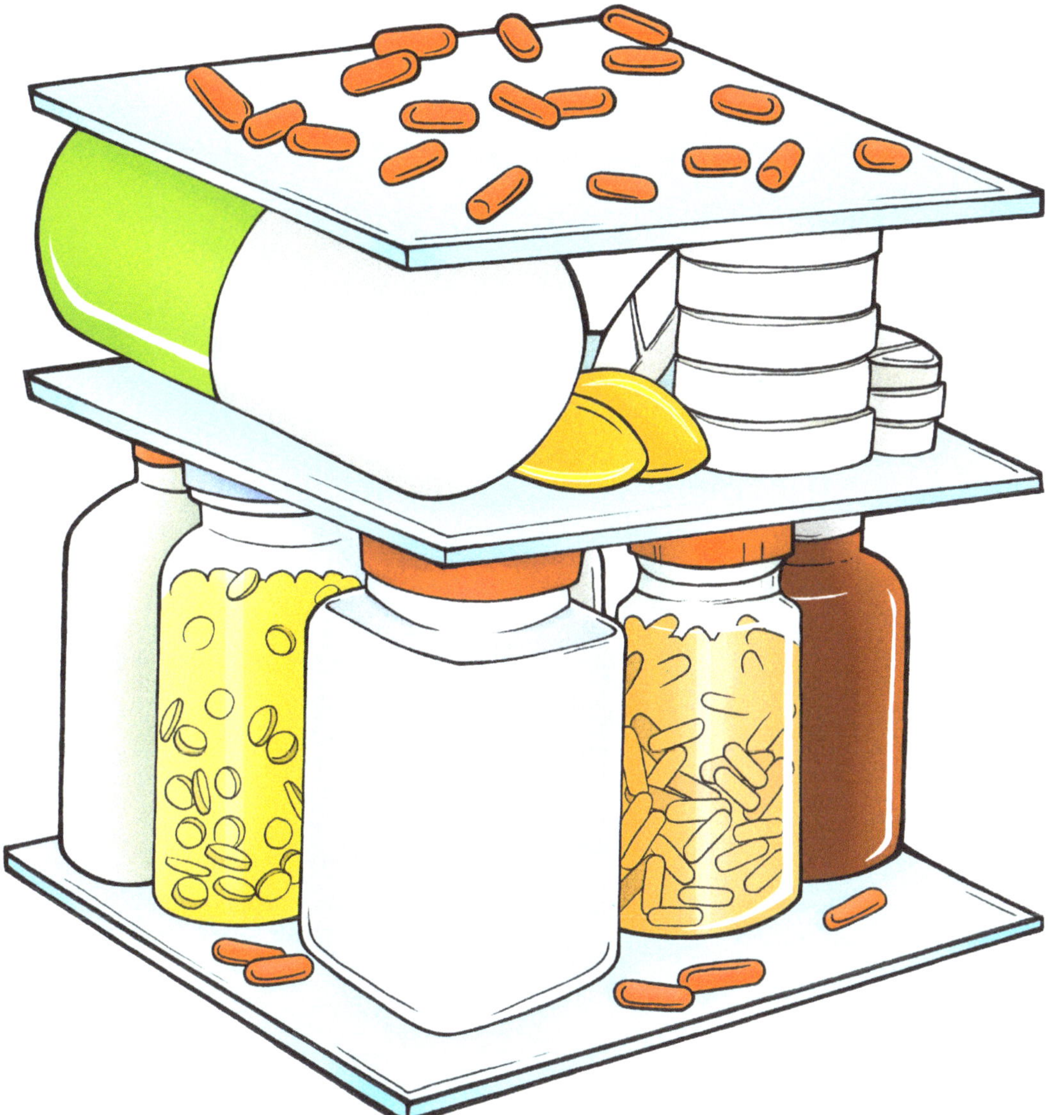

The company has superior lab supplies and solutions
And advancement came gradually; it was an evolution.
With hubby as president and her as CEO,
Neta Scientific expanded and continued to grow.

Offering innovation, quality, and a competitive price,
Neta is nimble, efficient, accessible, and precise.
With clients in pharma, biotech, and academia,
It’s no wonder they’re often featured in the media.

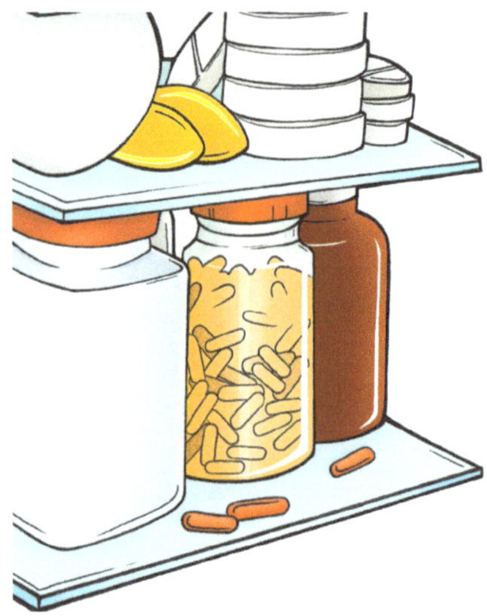

Janell Stephens
Camille Rose Naturals

Janell Stephens felt that it was her duty
To bring gourmet products to the world of beauty.
Her kitchen was where she brewed her first batches
To develop a cure for her children's rashes.

Their chronic eczema led her on a mission
To use natural substances to remedy their condition.
A vegan herself, her maxim was emphatic—
If it goes on the body, one should be able to ingest it.

Camille Rose Naturals was launched as a hobby
But the brand quickly grew; Janell was featured in Ebony.
The line includes products for both skin and hair,
Moisture-rich ingredients developed with care.

The products are handmade, vintage, and elegant—
Almond milks, honey, and fruits that are relevant
Hydrating blends to sweeten your routine,
Handcrafted with love so your hair stays pristine.

J C Sykes

90 Degree Construction

JC Sykes can wield a hammer,
Which is not often perceived as a symbol of glamour.
She uses a wrench, a saw, and chisels.
She works inside and outside, even when it drizzles.

90 Degree Construction is the name of her firm.
Excelling in carpentry as her clients can confirm
Trimming, flooring, framing, and such
Their prices are reasonable; they don't charge too much.

Though some tasks are daunting, JC doesn't squirm.
Her non-profit teaches girls that it's easy to earn
The lifestyle they want if they master their skills.
She named the organization Black Girls Build.

JC and her family are determined to win
And their business has thrived for years, nearly ten.
A building's foundation is most important for sure
So the Sykes' trained their son—the future's secure.

So now you've read all about seven amazing women.
Their success was hard-fought; it was never a given.
They overcame obstacles as they built their brands.
Their products and services are in high demand.

Two Janices, JC, Garnetta, and Bea,
Plus Valerie and Janell, their tenacity was the key.
With humble beginnings, not ashamed to tell,
They've risen to new heights determined to excel.

They are ordinary and special at the same time,

Which means you, too, can flourish, prosper, and climb.

No matter your background or station in life,

You can conquer all challenges, hurdles, and strife.

Believe in yourself is what they all say.

Your grit, guts, and courage will ultimately pave the way

For the path you'll leave for others to follow.

Your destiny will manifest a brighter tomorrow.

The Boss Women and Their Companies

Janice M. Adams

JMA Solutions

Location: Washington, DC

Website: www.jma-solutions.com

Valerie Daniels-Carter

V&J Holding Companies Inc.

Location: Milwaukee, WI

Website: www.vjfoods.com

Bea Dixon

The Honey Pot Company

Location: Atlanta, GA

Website: www.thehoneypot.co

Janice Bryant Howroyd

ActOne Group

Location: Torrance, CA

Website: www.actonegroup.com

Garnetta Sanders

Neta Scientific, Inc.

Location: Hainesport, NJ

Website: www.netascientific.com

Janelle Stephens

Camille Rose Naturals

Location: Macon, GA

Website: www.camillerose.com

J C Sykes

90 Degree Construction

Location: St. Louis, MO

Website: www.facebook.com/builtby90/

About the Author

Gwen Richardson has been a writer, entrepreneur and "boss woman" for decades. A graduate of Georgetown University, Ms. Richardson currently resides in Houston, Texas, with her husband, Willie.

Communication via email is welcome, including speaking and media requests.

Email the author at gwenrichardson123@gmail.com.
Visit the author's website: www.gwenrichardson.com
Facebook: @bosswomenthebook

www.ingramcontent.com/pod-product-compliance
Ingram Content Group UK Ltd.
Pitfield, Milton Keynes, MK11 3LW, UK
UKHW061031310726
14089UKWH00009B/195
* 9 7 8 1 7 3 7 4 4 9 6 1 4 *